D0601748

SCIENCE EXPLORER

MAGNETS

SUPER COOL
SCIENCE
EXPERIMENTS:
MAGNETS

by Christine Taylor-Butler

CHERRY LAKE PUBLISHING • ANN ARBOR, MICHIGAN

CHERRY LAKE
Publishing

A NOTE TO PARENTS AND TEACHERS: Please review the instructions for these experiments before your children do them. Be sure to help them with any experiments you do not think they can safely conduct on their own.

A NOTE TO KIDS: Be sure to ask an adult for help with these experiments when you need it. Always put your safety first!

Published in the United States of America by
Cherry Lake Publishing
Ann Arbor, Michigan
www.cherrylakepublishing.com

Content Editor: Robert Wolffe, EdD,
Professor of Teacher Education,
Bradley University, Peoria, Illinois

Book design and illustration: The Design Lab

Photo Credits: Cover and pages 1 and 28, ©Thomas Mounsey, used under
license from Shutterstock, Inc.; page 5, ©Alan_smithee/Dreamstime.com;
page 8, ©iStockphoto.com/Rocter; page 12, ©iStockphoto.com/colematt;
page 16, ©iStockphoto.com/dbuffoon; page 20, ©Mrbhughes/Dreamstime.
com; page 24, ©iStockphoto.com/NoDerog

Library of Congress Cataloging-in-Publication Data
Taylor-Butler, Christine.
  Super cool science experiments: Magnets / by Christine Taylor-Butler.
    p. cm.—(Science explorer)
  Includes bibliographical references and index. 42381102   1/10
  ISBN-13: 978-1-60279-530-3   ISBN-10: 1-60279-530-4 (lib. bdg.)
  ISBN-13: 978-1-60279-609-6   ISBN-10: 1-60279-609-2 (pbk.)
  1. Magnets—Experiments—Juvenile literature. I. Title. II. Title:
Magnets. III. Series.
  QC757.5.T39 2010
  538'.4078—dc22   2009004771

Cherry Lake Publishing would like to acknowledge the work
of The Partnership for 21st Century Skills. Please visit
www.21stcenturyskills.org for more information.

SCIENCE EXPLORER

MAGNETS

TABLE OF CONTENTS

Magic Magnets?

Take a look at your refrigerator door. Do you see any magnets? Maybe they are holding up your family's grocery list. How are magnets able to stay in place without falling to the floor? Is it magic?

Nope. But what you are witnessing is still amazing. It's an incredible force of nature called magnetism. Have you ever wondered how magnets work? If so, you are already one step closer to looking at the world around you through the eyes of a scientist. Can you believe that you can do experiments with things you already have at home? In this book, we'll learn how scientists think. We'll do that by experimenting with magnets. Plus, we'll learn many things and have fun along the way.

How many magnets are on your refrigerator door?

First Things First

Maquets come in many shapes and sizes

Scientists learn by studying something very carefully. For example, scientists who study magnets look for places where magnets are found within or on the earth. They see what objects stick to magnets and what objects do not. They notice that magnets can sometimes make common objects magnetic. They do experiments to see how magnets can be used to power machines or help us navigate Earth.

Good scientists take notes on everything they discover. They write down their observations. Sometimes those observations lead scientists to ask new questions. With new questions in mind, they design experiments to find the answers.

When scientists design experiments, they must think very clearly. The way they think about problems is often called the scientific method. What is the scientific method? It's a step-by-step way of finding answers to specific questions. The steps don't always follow the same pattern. Sometimes scientists change their minds. The process often works something like this:

Scientific method →

- **Step One:** A scientist gathers the facts and makes observations about one particular thing.
- **Step Two:** The scientist comes up with a question that is not answered by all the observations and facts.
- **Step Three:** The scientist creates a hypothesis. This is a statement of what the scientist thinks is probably the answer to the question.
- **Step Four:** The scientist tests the hypothesis. He or she designs an experiment to see whether the hypothesis is correct. The scientist does the experiment and writes down what happens.

- **Step Five:** The scientist draws a conclusion based on how the experiment turned out. The conclusion might be that the hypothesis is correct. Sometimes, though, the hypothesis is not correct. In that case, the scientist might develop a new hypothesis and another experiment.

In the following experiments, we'll see the scientific method in action. We'll gather some facts and observations about magnets. And for each experiment, we'll develop a question and a hypothesis. Next, we'll do an actual experiment to see if our hypothesis is correct. By the end of the experiment, we should know something new about magnets. Scientists, are you ready? Then let's get started!

Grab a pencil and a notebook!

Science Notes

Experiment #1

Let the Force

Be with You!

What kinds of objects are attracted to magnets?

First, let's gather some observations. What do you already know about magnets? You probably know that magnets have an invisible force that makes things stick to them. This means that magnets attract objects. For example, you may use magnets to stick papers to your refrigerator. In this case, the magnets are attracted to the refrigerator.

These observations lead us to a question: Do magnets attract all things or just some things? Our hypothesis for this first experiment is this: **Magnets only attract things that are made of metal.**

Now you can set up an experiment to test the hypothesis.

Here's what you'll need:

- A sheet of paper and a pencil to record your observations
- A horseshoe magnet or bar magnet
- A penny
- An iron nail
- A paper clip
- A steel ball bearing
- A dollar bill
- A small square of aluminum foil

You probably have most of these things at home.

Observations

Instructions:

1. Which objects do you think the magnet will attract? Draw a line down the middle of your paper. Write "Attracts" at the top of the left column. This means that objects stick to the magnet. Write "Does Not Attract" at the top of the right column.

2. Place the magnet on top of the penny and lift up. Does the penny stick to the magnet? If so, write "penny" in the left column. If not, write "penny" in the right column.

3. Repeat these steps with the nail, paper clip, and ball bearing.

4. Now fold the dollar bill in half. Hold the bill up by pinching the top edge of one of the folded halves. Let the other side hang down. Place the magnet close to the lower part. What happens? Try it with the aluminum foil.
   Do you get the same result?

Don't forget to record your results!

Attract | Does Not Attract

Conclusion:

After you've finished experimenting, look at your two-column chart. Which objects were attracted to the magnet? Do they have something in common? What do you notice about the items that were not attracted to the magnet? What can you conclude from this experiment? Does a magnet attract all types of metal?

Why didn't the magnet pick up the penny? It's made of metal, right? Magnets are only attracted to certain metals, including iron, steel, and nickel. Old pennies are made of copper. New pennies are made of copper and zinc. Those metals are not attracted to a magnet. There is one exception. In 1943, the government needed copper to use in the war. That year, pennies were made from steel instead of copper.

Did it surprise you that the magnet made the dollar move? Magnets are not attracted to paper. So why does the dollar have magnetic properties? Dollar bills are printed with ink that has iron in it. The magnet attracts the iron particles in the ink.

Experiment #2
Do Opposites
Really Attract?

Magnets have a north pole and a south pole.

In Experiment #1, we learned that magnets are only attracted to certain kinds of metals. A scientist might wonder if magnets can do other things. Perhaps the scientist might ask this question: If magnets can attract certain types of objects, can magnets also repel objects? This means to push them away. You may have noticed that the bar magnet has two letters on it: N and S. These are called the north and south poles of the magnet.

So here's a new hypothesis to test: **Magnets always attract other magnets.**

Here's what you'll need:
- 2 bar magnets with ends marked "S" and "N"
- 2 refrigerator magnets
- A sheet of paper and a pencil

Your teacher may have some bar magnets you can borrow.

Instructions:
1. Place the magnets far apart on the table. Take one bar magnet and place the end labeled "S" on a refrigerator magnet. Do the two magnets stick together? Now place the end labeled "N" on the refrigerator magnet. What happens? Write your observations on a sheet of paper.

What do you think will happen?

2. Put the bar magnets to the side for a few minutes. Place the two refrigerator magnets next to each other. Do they stick together? What if you turn one magnet upside down? What happens if you place the front of one magnet against the back of the other? Why do you think that is?

3. Now put the bar magnets on the table in front of you. Place the end of the first magnet marked "S" next to the end of the second magnet marked "N." Did they attract or repel? Write it down. A good scientist keeps track of everything. Does this prove your hypothesis?

4. Turn one bar magnet around so that the "N" side is facing the "N" side of the other bar magnet. What happens? Try pushing them together. Can you do it? What happens if you try to put the two sides marked "S" together? Now try putting different sides together. Do you get the same results? What do you think this means?

Conclusion:

When scientists make a hypothesis, they are using what they know to make a prediction, or educated guess. But sometimes the answer isn't what they expected. Did you get the results you expected? If not, that's okay. It's how discoveries are made. In this case, when magnets with opposite poles are placed together, they attract. When magnets with the same poles are placed together, they push away. Why don't refrigerator magnets work the same way? These flat magnets are created using a special process. The surface is made of magnetic materials arranged in a row: NSNSNS. Any type of magnet will stick to it, and it can stick to itself.

In Japan, Germany, and France, scientists are using their knowledge of how magnets attract and repel to build high-speed trains. These trains do not have engines. Instead, the trains float above a magnetic track. Electricity is used to change the track's magnetic energy to push or pull the train. New trains can travel as fast as 300 miles per hour (483 kilometers per hour).

Experiment #3
Share the Power

↖ How many objects do you think one magnet can pick up?

In our last experiment, we learned that magnets are powerful. But a magnetic field is invisible. So it is not easy to see how much power a magnet contains. A scientist might wonder how far the field stretches. Can a magnet pick up more than one item at a time? Can it attract objects from far away? Here are two hypotheses you can test:

Hypothesis #1: Magnets can pick up more than one object at a time.

Hypothesis #2: Magnets can pick up items without touching them.

Here's what you'll need:
- A pencil and paper to record your observations
- A bar or horseshoe magnet
- 10 paper clips
- 10 safety pins
- 10 screw bolts
- A ruler

Instructions:
1. Put each set of objects in separate piles. Place the magnet on top of the paper clips. How many paper clips were you able to pick up?

2. What do you think would happen if you added more paper clips to the pile? Try it!
3. Remove the paper clips, and wave the magnet over the safety pins. What happens?
4. Try the bolts. Can you pick them all up? Why do you think that is?
5. Let's test the second hypothesis. Put your objects back into separate piles. Stand a ruler upright next to the paper clips.
6. Put the magnet 3 inches (7.6 centimeters) above the pile. Can you attract anything from this distance?
7. Put the magnet 2 inches (5 cm) above the pile. What happens?
8. Try putting the magnet 1 inch (2.5 cm) from the pile.
9. Repeat steps 5 through 8 with the safety pins.
10. Repeat steps 5 through 8 with the bolts. Do you have to get closer when the objects get heavier?
11. You can carry your testing a step further. Place your paper clips in a single row, end to end. Use the magnet to pick up the end of the first paper clip. Now place the free end of the paper clip next to the second paper clip. Does the first paper clip stick

How long is your paper clip chain?

to the second clip to form a chain? How many paper clips can you pick up this way?

12. Repeat step 11 with the pins and again with the bolts. Does weight or size make a difference?

13. Finally, try to make a chain of different items: one bolt, one safety pin, and one paper clip. What happens? Write down all of your observations.

Conclusion:

You've seen that a magnet can pick up more than one item even if the magnet isn't touching it. How is that possible? Metal, along with everything else, is made up of tiny parts called atoms. These atoms are arranged in a random pattern. The ends of each atom have an electrical charge. When a magnet attracts an object, the atoms of that object line up so the electrical charge faces the same direction. For a few seconds, that object becomes a magnet. It is not very strong, but it can use its power to pick up another object. The second object has even less power. This keeps going until there isn't enough energy left to pick up another item. If you use a more powerful magnet, you can pick up more items before you run out of "power."

If a magnet is strong enough and lifts up an object for a long enough length of time, something interesting happens. The object will be able to act like a magnet even when it is not in contact with the magnet. But this effect is temporary.

Experiment #4
Which Way Is North?

← Do you know why a compass needle points north?

A compass is a useful tool. It can help to keep you from getting lost when you are camping. Let's start with what you know about a compass. A compass has a single hand that spins like a clock. But unlike a clock, this hand or needle stops spinning when it points north.

How does a compass work? From Experiment #1, we know that magnets are attracted to some objects. And we know from Experiment #3 that a magnet can turn an ordinary object into a magnet as long as that object is touching a magnet. But how does a compass know where to point? Let's experiment to find out. Here's a new hypothesis: **Earth has magnetic properties.**

Here's what you'll need:

- 2 large sewing needles
- 2 clear water glasses that are the same size (Make sure the sewing needles can fit sideways inside the glass without touching the sides.)
- A ruler
- 8 inches (20.3 cm) of string
- A pencil
- A bar magnet
- Water
- A small cork

Instructions:

1. Measure the height of 1 glass with a ruler. Divide that number by 2. Record that number.

2. Tie one end of your string around the middle of 1 needle. Now attach the other end of the string around the middle of the pencil. Make sure the length of the string between the needle and the pencil is equal or nearly equal to the number you recorded.

3. Rub one end of the bar magnet over the needle. Always rub it in the same direction from left to right. Repeat 30 times.

4. When you are finished, place the needle inside the glass, resting the pencil on top of the glass. What happens when the needle stops spinning? What direction is it pointing? Record your observations.

5. Fill the second glass with water. Place the cork in the water.

6. Rub the magnet over the second needle. Then set the needle on top of the cork. Does the second needle point in the same direction as the first? Record your observations.

7. Let the experiment rest for an hour. Are the needles still pointing in the same direction? Record your observations.

8. Recheck the experiment in the morning. Do you get the same results?

Conclusion:

Why do you think the needles pointed in the direction they did? Which way do you think is north? Do you think that Earth has magnetic properties?

You may want to try some variations of your experiment. Try rubbing the needle 50 times or 100 times. Does the magnetic charge last longer? Can you think of other variations to explore?

Imagine that a giant stick runs through the center of Earth. One end would come out at the North Pole. The other end would come out at the South Pole. This is called an axis. Earth spins around it. The center of Earth is solid iron. It is covered with a layer of melted iron. We know that magnets are attracted to iron. When Earth spins, the liquid moves. This creates a magnetic field.

However, many people don't know that the planet's magnetic fields are flipped. The North Pole is actually charged like the south side of your magnet. The South Pole is charged like the north side of your magnet.

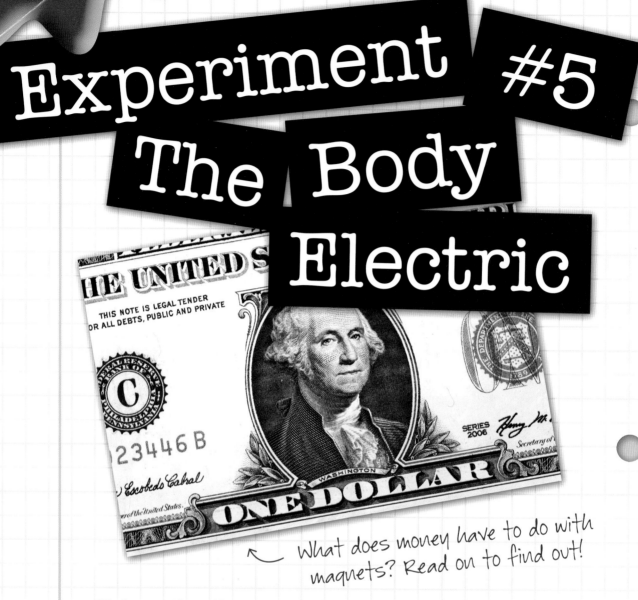

Experiment #5
The Body Electric

← What does money have to do with magnets? Read on to find out!

We know that Earth acts like a giant magnet. Some metals have a magnetic charge. Even the ink used to print our money has magnetic properties. But what about you? Does your body have magnetic properties as well? If it did, wouldn't your magnets stick to your hands while you performed these experiments? Let's try a hypothesis: **The human body contains substances with magnetic properties.**

Here's what you'll need:

- ¼ cup of an iron-fortified cereal, such as Total
- A bowl
- A spoon
- The strongest magnet you can find
- 4 resealable plastic bags
- A hammer
- A cup of warm water
- A magnifying glass
- An iron-fortified adult vitamin

Look for cereal that has 100% of the daily value for iron.

Instructions:

1. Put 1 tablespoon of the cereal in a bowl. Mash it with the spoon until it is broken into tiny pieces. Place the magnet close to the cereal. What happens? Write down your observations.

2. Now pour the remaining cereal into a plastic bag. Close the bag tightly. Gently crush the cereal with your hands until it is broken into tiny pieces. Lay the bag on a table or counter, and tap it gently with a hammer, breaking the cereal into a powder.
3. Pour the powder into a different plastic bag. Add 3 tablespoons of warm water. Mix well, until it is a soupy mixture. Seal the bag.
4. Slide the magnet along the bottom of the bag. Do you see anything unusual? Try looking through a magnifying glass as you slowly move the magnet. Write down your observations.
5. Slowly rub the magnet all over the bag of soupy cereal. Lift the magnet about $1/8$ inch above the bag, and move it from side to side about $1/2$ inch. What happens? Do tiny black particles of iron collect near your magnet? Move the magnet to a clean section of the bag. Can you see the iron now?

Watch carefully to see what happens!

6. Repeat this experiment using a crushed vitamin and 1 tablespoon of warm water. Use the magnifying glass to get a close-up view.

Conclusion:

Think about what you observed. Which has more iron: the cereal or the vitamin? What happens to the iron when you eat the cereal or vitamin? Does your body have magnetic properties?

The human body needs iron to keep its red blood cells healthy. Iron helps the blood carry oxygen. But how do you get iron into your body? Tiny amounts of iron are found in many foods you eat. Some companies add iron to foods such as cereals. Look at the nutrition facts listed on the cereal box. Are you surprised at how little there is? You don't need very much.

Experiment #6
Do It Yourself!

← You can do many different experiments with bar magnets.

How about running a classic experiment on your own? Try to discover which part of a bar magnet has the strongest magnetic force. Where do you think the force might be the strongest? At the poles? Along the sides? Near the center? Come up with a hypothesis.

For your experiment, you'll need a bar magnet, a sheet of paper, and iron filings. You can find iron filings at a school supply store or a science supply store. Your teacher may also have some you can use. Place the bar magnet on a table. Lay the paper over the bar magnet. Sprinkle the iron filings on the paper over the area with the magnet. Slightly move the paper back and forth over the magnet. How do the iron filings react? Do you see any shapes or patterns? Do more iron filings move toward certain areas? What does this tell you about the strength of the magnetic field in these areas?

Okay, scientists! Now you know many new things about magnets. You learned through your observations and experiments. You even discovered that tiny magnetic particles are inside of you! So what's next? That's up to you!

You can learn a lot with a magnet and some iron filings.

GLOSSARY

axis (AK-sis) a real or imaginary line that runs through the center of an object, and around which the object turns

compass (KUHM-puhs) a tool that shows the direction of Earth's magnetic field

conclusion (kuhn-KLOO-zhuhn) a final decision, thought, or opinion

experiments (ehks-PEHR-ih-ments) scientific processes used to discover information

force (FORSE) an invisible energy that can cause something to move

hypothesis (hy-POTH-uh-sihss) a logical guess about what will happen in an experiment

magnetic field (mag-NEH-tic FEELD) an area around a magnet in which the magnet has the power to attract or repel

method (METH-uhd) a way of doing something

observations (ob-zur-VAY-shuhnz) things that are seen or noticed with one's senses

poles (POLZ) the ends of a magnet or a planet's axis

FOR MORE INFORMATION

BOOKS

Jeffers, Fred. *Mondo Magnets: 40 Attractive (and Repulsive) Devices & Demonstrations.* Chicago: Chicago Review Press, 2007.

Levine, Shar, and Leslie Johnstone. *Magnet Power!* New York: Sterling Pub., 2006.

Royston, Angela. *Magnetic and Nonmagnetic.* Chicago: Heinemann Library, 2009.

WEB SITES

Exploratorium: Science Snacks
www.exploratorium.edu/snacks/
Experiments with magnets and other fun stuff

Magnet Lab: Try This at Home
www.magnet.fsu.edu/education/students/activities/trythisathome.html
Several fun and easy experiments with magnets

Magnet Man: Cool Experiments with Magnets
www.coolmagnetman.com/magindex.htm
Many fun facts and experiments with magnets

INDEX

About the → Author

Christine Taylor-Butler is a freelance author with degrees in both civil engineering and art and design from the Massachusetts Institute of Technology (MIT). When she is not writing, she is reading, drawing, or looking for unusual new science ideas to write about. She is the author of more than 40 fiction and nonfiction books for children.